IMAGINE
PROSPER

YOU ARE THE AUTHOR OF YOUR WORLD

IMAGINE PROSPER

YOU ARE THE AUTHOR OF YOUR WORLD

SANDY CORSO
PEACEFUL DAILY PUBLISHING

Copyright © 2020 Sandy Corso

All rights reserved.

No part of this book may be reproduced, copied, stored or transmitted in any form or by any means – graphic, electronic or mechanical, including photocopying, without the prior written permission of Peaceful Daily Publishing, except where permitted by law.

Library of Congress Control Number: 2019950972

ISBN 978-0-9982579-6-9
EISBN 978-0-9982579-7-6

Cover and book design by Perseus-Design.com

Published by Peaceful Daily Publishing
www.peacefuldaily.com

Printed in the United States of America.

First Edition

10 9 8 7 6 5 4 3 2 1

Dedicated to myself

because I am the author
of my world…

> "EVERYTHING YOU CAN IMAGINE IS REAL."
>
> PABLO PICASSO

CONTENTS

Introduction	xi
Epiphany	1
3 Simple Steps	3
Ponder	9
Gratitude	67
About the Author	69

INTRODUCTION

If this book has found you, I believe you have been chosen to receive this knowledge—just as I have been.

Many years ago, I made a commitment to myself: To do good work that made the world a better place. I am proud to say I stuck to that commitment and did not waver. It was not always easy. There were successes and there were failures, but I never gave up. I feel the struggles were there to keep me seeking wisdom. I was pushed, and now I have some insight I can share with others.

I am constantly looking for the answers to life. I am on a quest to figure out what life is about and how we can do our best—how we can make ourselves and the world a better place. Living a happy, prosperous and loving life has been, and always will be, my mission.

I always knew I would have an epiphany one day and figure it all out. I am finally inspired to share with the world.

WE CAN ALL HAVE ANYTHING WE WANT. WE ARE MEANT TO PROSPER.

My happy place is nature. When I was ready to share, I sat down on a stone in my yard, surrounded by the magical trees and the warm wind and started writing this book.

I can't begin to tell you the profound effect the ideas within these pages have had on me. Slowly but surely, I have been applying them to my life, and things are changing in magical ways.

IMAGINE PROSPER. Although small in size, the words and thoughts are powerful. It could possibly have a profound effect on your life. It quite possibly may help you make all your dreams come true.

An even more important idea is this…If we can use this knowledge collectively as a world and really focus on things like healing our world and our planet, we can shape our lives forever.

Take your time. Read these ideas slowly. Ponder them. You may reread this book many times over. I felt no

INTRODUCTION

need to write a 500-page book. The ideas are simple and need not be complicated with redundancy and over explanation.

Feel free to message me and let me know your thoughts and experiences with the ideas contained within this book.

Peace, Love & Happiness,

Sandy

EPIPHANY

Every single thing that we have created was first imagined.

You must understand this magical creating power resides in you and in everyone. I personally call it my Divine power, my God power. You may call it something else. You may call it a Universal or Higher power. It does not matter what you call it. Just acknowledge it is a divine power within you.

The way you choose to experience everything that is in your life now is the product of your mind. You are creating your existence with your imagination, which includes thoughts, words, and feelings.

I believe the divine spirit within us is constantly operating and giving us whatever we imagine. It is divine imagination at work. When we daydream about our desires, we are creating. When we worry, we are creating. We are always creating, no matter what. You can have anything you want in your life, and I do mean *anything*.

When looking at your life, there is no one else to blame, there is no one else to thank; it is all you. Your imagination is constantly at work, even when you don't realize it. It is changing the way you look at the world and altering the way you live. Grab hold of your imagination and use it to create the life you want.

3 SIMPLE STEPS

DECIDE WHAT YOU WANT

The first thing you must do is to decide what you want to create, all the desires, aspirations and everything you want for yourself. Don't rush to decide what is important. Spend time and think about what you really want. Don't hold back. I believe our desires are coming from our divine power, our soul expressions and they are our destiny; what we are meant to do and accomplish in this life. We are all here for a reason and I believe our desires hold the key.

Be bold and honest and list everything you want to create and accomplish.

This list will obviously change over time. That is normal and a sign of growth and expansion.

IMAGINE WITH FEELING

Once you know what you want, you must begin to use your imagination to create it.

Morning, noon and night you must play out scenes of your desires using your imagination accompanied by your senses and feelings.

For instance, sit in silence and play out, in your imagination, everything you want. Make sure to use your senses to make it as real as possible. Hear the voices of what others will say, feel the feeling of touching the very things you want to create, smell the ocean breeze if you want a house by the sea, really feel the things you are imagining. Use your senses and feelings to make your imaginations as vivid as possible.

FAITH

When you go about your day you must accept your imaginations as truth. You must have unwavering faith that what you are imagining is already here in your life. You must act as if all the things you want in your life are already here. Always have faith that your desires are real no matter what.

Unwavering faith is the key.

PONDER

PONDER

You must understand that your imagination is your one and only creative power. You can use it to create anything in your life. It is the prerequisite to everything...

The answer to every single problem contained within this life is your magical imagination.

PONDER

Think of everything you imagine as a command to the world.

The only place your enemies live is in your imagination. If you think the world is mean, mean people will show up.

PONDER

Everything in your life is there because you asked for it either by desire or fear.

There are no negative thoughts all thoughts have a positive outcome. Meaning, all thoughts create something. It may be something good or bad. Either way all thoughts manifest something.

PONDER

Success and failure are both created in the imagination.

Use your imagination for others in a kind and loving way. All the good you imagine for others comes back to you.

PONDER

I remember when I was... (poor, sick, depressed) is a great way of imagining your problems are no longer showing up.

Ignore the facts of life and assume you are what you want to be, because everything stems from imaginal activity.

PONDER

Make sure not to think OF what you want. Think and imagine FROM your desire.

Imagine and focus on the end result (what you ultimately want). Don't worry about figuring it all out or how you will make it happen. Plant the seed; it will grow. Your desires will guide you as to what to do so you can make it happen.

PONDER

Do not blame others for anything. Everything happening in your world was created by you.

If you want to hold on to something you must hold onto it only in your imagination. Fear of loss will take it away.

PONDER

Share these lessons with everyone. The more people understand these ideas, the more good will be created and the world will be a better place.

Talking about your problems? You will perpetuate them all the more.

PONDER

The world is a mirror always reflecting back to you what is going on in your imagination.

Paying attention to all the bad things going on in the world and believing it only creates more of it.

PONDER

Our imagination is a magical tool. Our desires are our destiny. Doubt is the devil.

If others have wronged you, forgive them. When we forgive, we let go and stop dwelling on the negative. Remembering what you forgave is bringing it back. FORGET all wrongs done to you.

PONDER

When dealing with other people focus on their good qualities and traits. Ignore all the things that bother you. Do not worry and fret about them. The more attention you pay to them the more they show up for you.

Don't you feel better knowing now that you are divine power?

PONDER

Inspiration comes from the depths of your soul. Never ignore what inspires you, it is your divine guidance.

If you want others to behave differently, imagine them as you would like them to be. There is no need to tell them what to do. Use your imagination to create how you want them to show up for you.

PONDER

I am what I want to be. Fall asleep with it being true. The moment before you fall asleep is a magical time and the perfect time to use your imagination in a loving way for yourself.

You are what you want to be. Make sure you believe it at all times with blind faith.

PONDER

Whenever we blame others, we are giving our power away. If you want to be powerful assume responsibility for everything in your life.

Life is always, beyond a shadow of a doubt, displaying what you are creating in your imagination.

PONDER

When you imagine your loved ones, imagine them receiving what they want.

Controlling your feelings is very important. Never entertain an undesirable feeling.

PONDER

Do not think/worry/imagine what you do not want done to you.

Change your feelings, change your life.

PONDER

Dare to have it all. Dream and imagine all the magnificent things you want.

Never dwell on the imperfections of yourself or others. Remember we are all one.

Your awareness of things is the reason for everything that is and will show up in your life.

Saying it is not possible is a sin; everything is possible with your divine imagination.

PONDER

Life should not be a struggle; it should be a surrender.

Everything in the world is either use or misuse of imagination.

PONDER

Freedom and forgiveness are linked. If you want freedom, forgive everything that is holding you back.

I believe my desires are wishes from my divine guidance and my imagination the divine helping me get where I need to go.

PONDER

Daily revisions are extremely important. If you have a bad day, when you go to sleep at night rewrite in your imagination anything that happened in the day that you did not like.

Everyone you meet is yourself made visible. What you expect of others is what shows up. Expect and only focus on the good qualities of others.

PONDER

Life is so much easier when you just expect others to be their best. Forgive and be kind to everyone.

Focus on LOVE and loving actions always.

PONDER

Withdraw your attention from anything negative that will not make you happy.

Imagination is more important than knowledge.

PONDER

Live in your imagination as much as possible.

Create your days.

When we help and forgive others we are actually helping and forgiving ourselves.

PONDER

Inner conversations play a role in your creating. Everything you are whispering to yourself in your mind is creating what is showing up in your life.

What is going on in your mind is way more important that what is going on in the physical world.

PONDER

Imagination is a spiritual sensation.

All the answers come from the depth of your own soul, which really is a divine and magical force.

PONDER

The most important thing you can discipline is your feelings.

Your mind is the new frontier. Your imagination trumps everything.

PONDER

The world needs me, and it needs me to be the best I can be. The world needs you and needs you to be the best you can be.

GRATITUDE

I have an immense amount of gratitude for the teachers throughout my life; my amazing parents, my beautiful kids and of course my love, my husband.

There have been other teachers as well. They have all had a huge impact on my life and the messages contained within this book.

My journey has been nothing less than magical. Over the years, I have had many amazing opportunities and was able to spend time with some of the greatest thought-leaders of our time!

I have done yoga classes with Russell Simmons, discussed world peace with Michael Franti, drank green juice with Dr. Wayne Dyer, talked inspiration with Louise Hay and even watched in awe as the Dalai Lama captivated crowds.

There have also been other teachers like Neville Goddard, Abraham Hicks, Oprah Winfrey and Panache Desai that inspired my knowledge seeking journey. We are living in a triumphant time; so many amazing teachers.

Throughout the years, I have also had some really cool experiences: rain dances, raw vegan retreats, crystal healing, meditations in nature, barefoot hiking—all kinds of things to learn about myself and the spiritual world.

Without the knowledge of these souls and my miraculous experiences this book would not be possible.

Xo Sandy

ABOUT THE AUTHOR

Sandy Corso is extremely passionate about spreading inspiration and healthy living ideas. Her desire is to manifest a world founded on principles of compassion, well-being and making the world a better place!

Sandy has worked in the healthy living/spiritual world for many years.

Blogging for the healthy living section of The Huffington Post for almost 10 years was a natural conduit for her words. That eventually led her to write her best-selling book Peace Salad published in 2013.

In 2009 she founded Peaceful Daily. Peaceful Daily began as a healthy living blog and later morphed into a publishing house helping other healthy living influencers bring their inspiring words to the world.

Sandy currently lives in Connecticut with her husband Gary, two teenage kids Topanga and Jaco, Zuma the dog and Wheatie the cat.

You can keep up with Sandy on all social media platforms at @sandycorso or visit her at sandycorso.com.

GRATITUDE PAGES

GRATITUDE PAGES

GRATITUDE PAGES

GRATITUDE PAGES

GRATITUDE PAGES

www.ingramcontent.com/pod-product-compliance
Lightning Source LLC
Chambersburg PA
CBHW051602010526
44118CB00023B/2793